FRANK HARRINGTON'S

KRISTMISS BOOK

1860 – 1900

Frank Harrington's

KRISTMISS BOOK

Edited by Nelson Ball

Photographs by R.R. Sallows

THE MERCURY PRESS

The Mercury Press gratefully acknowledges the financial assistance of the Canada Council, the Ontario Arts Council, and the Government of Ontario through the Ontario Publishing Centre.

Reuben R. Sallows' photographs, from the R.R. Sallows Collection of the Ontario Ministry of Agriculture and Food, Visual Services Department, are used by permission. Prints prepared by Terry A. McDonald.

Thanks to Lynn Campbell, Ontario Agricultural Museum, and to Peter Hume and Cary Little, Ontario Ministry of Agriculture and Food. The Press extends special thanks to Nelson Ball.

Cover design: Ted Glaszewski
Printed on acid-free paper at Guelph, Ontario, by Amerpsand Printing

CANADIAN CATALOGUING IN PUBLICATION
Harrington, Frank, d. 1900
Frank Harrington's Kristmiss book
ISBN 1-55128-006-X
1. Harrington, Frank, d. 1900. 2. Agriculture -
Ontario - History - 19th century. 3. Farmers -
Ontario - Biography. I. Ball, Nelson, 1942-
II. Title. III. Title: Kristmiss book.
S417.H3A3 1993   630'.92   C93-094767-3

PREFACE

THIS IS THE PERSONAL DIARY, with each entry made on Christmas Day, of a pioneer farmer in the area known as the Queen's Bush (now the Ontario counties of Grey, Huron and Bruce).

The diary spans a period of forty years. In very few words, the author presents a vivid and dramatic account of the events in his and his family's lives. The account reveals the satisfactions and the many hardships encountered by the people who settled in the area at the time.

In 1971, I first read the text of this diary in the Bruce County Historical Society *Year Book*. I was struck by the poignancy of the narrative and the directness, brevity and continuity of its presentation. The prose has incidental literary qualities I found appealing—its rhythm, the occurrence of run-on and repetition, and the cobbled spelling.

The *Year Book* version of the text had line breaks determined by the size of the pages on which it was printed. I re-typed the text, changing the line breaks to elicit and reinforce the rhythm and imagery I found in the prose.

My intention, in 1971, was to publish the diary in book form. However, other commitments prevented me from pursuing the project. In 1990, I showed my transcription of the diary to Don and Beverley Daurio whose interest revived the project.

Nelson Ball
Toronto, 1971 / Paris, 1993

FRANK HARRINGTON'S

KRISTMISS BOOK

1860 – 1900

Kristmiss 18 hunderd and 60

am alivin with the Conlys till I git me shack up
I come hear on the twenty firs day of Septembur and I have got 1 hundrud akers

1861

sot up a log house—and cleared tenn akers—put it in weet—it looks well
turble cold
was chased out of the clearen by a pack of wolves yesturday
Katie Conly bakes for me

1862

bot a ox team an built a stable
weet turned first rate
Katie Conly give me a pair of soxe for a Kristmiss present

1863

wolves et a cow onto me las winter
summer frost killed my weet
I cut me foot fearfull with the ax las week—Katie Conly comes over every noon an fixes me foot an feeds the oxen

1864

cleared 80 akers
took 200 hundurd bags taters down to Gelf bot Katie Conly the makins of a new dress

1865

had fever and agy all summer—wood hav dide if it hadnt bin for Katie Conly

1866

Katie Conly is a goin with another fella—when I had a loggin bee she never come aneer she say o you go git the widder Malkom

1867

shes agoin with that fella yit

1868

tuk Katie down to Gelf and Married her just after harvest—everything is hunky dory now

1869

trow a tree onto one of me oxen en hurt the other
bot me a horse

1870

baby come on June the second
horse died onto me
bot me a yoke of steers

1871

baby died march the ate
traded the steers an forty cord of wood fer a team of horses

1872

got burnd out by a fores fire las augus—los most every thing
Katie frets a good deal
am gettin out lumber for a frame house next spring

1873

put up a bully frame
four rooms upstairs an a baby come on July 12
at Oldbridge town thur was a famus battel an many a man lade on the ground an the cannons they did ratel

1874

John Burnford er Mowat made me a magustrat—I never thot ide live to see this day

1875

was elected scule trustee—I pass the plate on Sundays

1876

little Andy Harington was born on tent of November
the scule master is bordin with us—hes givin me lesins on the sli

1877

wen to a politicle picknick at Gelf—Sir Jon Mickdonald shuck hands with me an says hows little Andy—Howd he no little Andys name was little Andy

1878

little Jack Harington was born May the six—never seen Katie look better
put up a new barn

1879

bot fifty akers of old man Conly its mostly bush
took little Andy Harington with me for a grist the other day—he held the lines an said git up there horsey just as plane as plane

1880

Katie was poorly all summer had two doctors—she went to Toronto for a consultashun its goin to cost me a pile of muny it cost me moren them 50 akers
childrun all had the measles
Mary Ellen shes goin to schule

1881

went to law with big Jim Swarts bout a line fence
hes onto me mordun ten inches in some places—he clames 2 pine trees and an oke its a white on to
them trees is on my propurty an ile fite him as long as I hev a york shillin

1882

bete Swarts at the Gelf assizes but hes peeled the case
what the little schulemem calls the stork brot us a baby gurl six weeks ago
Ime goin to call her Susan Ann after mother—Katie wants to call her Murtil—the little schulemem wants us to call her Ofeelya
but shes goin to be Susan Ann and dont you forgit it neither

1883

Mary Ellen is in the second buke—I am a proud man this day—little Andy goes to schule in fine wether
Jack swallied a marbel and we had a dikens of a time
ive got offle stout—beleve ive got the assma—me breth is so short
Susan Ann is just the pitcher of our fokes—the naybers say shes the ded image of me

1884

Mary Ellen kin play the Maydens Prayer an Bonny crosn the Alps on the organ
i was lected reeve last January
Swarts loses his peel
baby Susan Ann and Little Jack watch for Christmas

1885

was selected reeve by acklimashun—am goin to run for parliment someday
Susan Ann is groin turrble fast

1886

little Jack Harington fell of a teeter last summer and broke his leg and a coller bone
the schulemaster whaled little Andy this fall—the darn skunk said little Andy was sassie
ile run that fellow out of the sekshun woodant i jus like to see him lay a hand on Susan Ann

1887

horses ran away with little Andy an smashed the binder all to smithyreens
little Andy was at a shiveree last june and come home with 15 burd-shot in his hide
wen i was shur he wood git better i tole him serve you rite Andy—I no how to bring up childurn in the rite way

1888

Katie dide las augus she was sensible to the las her las words was look out fer little Andy an Susan Ann
Susan Anns all rite an sos we Andy theve for got moren them other childurn will ever no
Ime lonely sometimes—I wish ide bin better to Katie

1889

theres a gurl on the fifth conseshun is sooin we Andy for $2000.00
Andy has skipped out to Michigan—I never thot ide live to see this day

1890

pade the gurl $500.00 to settle it an Mary Ellen shes tuk the baby fer to raise—I never thot ide live to see this day

1891

the baby looks like my poor Kate thats ded an gone—I wish I was with her—I never thot ide live to see this day

1892

bot a peana for Susan Ann—shes the comfort of my life
Andy is keepin saloon in Sagganaw—I never thot ide live to see this day

1893

Bill Malkom wants to marry my Mary Ellen—hes after my property thats what hes after
Mary Ellen seems to cotton to him

1894

Bill an Mary Ellen got marid
I give em the Conly 50 to live on theyl git along you bet

1895

wee Andy was killed in barrom fite in Bay City Michigan las summer
I went over an brot the body home for buryal—I never thot ide live to see this day

1896

Jack and Will hev hired a fella named Tom Smith to help on the farm

1897

made my will—settled a $1000.00 on Andys baby—poor Andy I cant forget him

1898

didnt like the way the hired man an Susan Ann carried on pade him off
he jus went an hired on the next farm I wish Katie was alive

1899

Mary Ellen says that folks is talkin about my Susan Ann—I wish that poor Katie was alive

1900

Susan Ann ran away with the hired man—what have I done that I hev lived to see this day

Mary Ellen added the following lines:

Christmas 1900 10:00 a.m. Found poor father dead in his chair with the pen in his hand he was a good father to me. Susan Ann is coming home—he left her in Detroit. God help us all.

—Mary Ellen Malcolm.

A NOTE ON THE PHOTOGRAPHER

REUBEN R. SALLOWS was born in Huron County, Ontario, in 1855. Searching for a job in 1876, he sat for a photograph in a studio in Goderich, and was offered employment as the photographer's assistant.

In 1881, he set up his own studio in Goderich, where he took the formal studio portraits common at the time.

His innovations— taking his cameras into the countryside, and creating powerful compositions in black

and white— altered Canadian photography. Sallows' talent and professionalism made him internationally famous. His clients included newspapers and magazines in Canada and the United States, as well as the Canadian government.

With his wife, Flora McKinnon, Sallows raised three children in Goderich. He died at age 82 in a car accident on his way to take photographs at a church camp.

AFTERWORD

THIS DIARY HAS BEEN PUBLISHED at least twice previously: in the Dec. 19, 1963 issue of the *Family Herald* and in the 1971 issue of the Bruce County Historical Society *Year Book*.

The *Family Herald* appearance is headed by an illustration which incorporates the title "Kristmiss Diary 1860......1900" followed by an editor's note which reads:

> This unique diary published here came into the possession of Donald McDonald of Cooksville, Ont. It was kept by a pioneer of the Queen's Bush (comprised of Ontario's counties of Huron, Bruce, and Grey) whom we have here called Frank Harrington, and who went to the region in 1860 to hew out a home for himself in the wilderness. Each entry was made on Christmas Day at the end of the year. Names have been changed, for obvious reasons.

In 1990, I wrote to H. Gordon Green who had been the editor of the *Family Herald* in 1963. I asked him about the origin of this piece and for permission to republish it. He responded that it "...was purchased by myself for a *Family Herald* Christmas issue.... I do not of course have any record of who submitted this to the *Family*

Herald. I think I could personally give [you] permission to use same in any way [you] choose."

The version published in the 1971 issue of the Bruce County Historical Society *Year Book* carries the same title, illustration and editor's note as in the *Family Herald*. Preceding the editor's note is the line "Donated [contributed] by Gordon F. Hepburn...." Mrs. Olive Hepburn confirmed in 1990 that the source for the *Year Book* version had been "a clipping from a newspaper or a magazine which my husband saved."

In the *Year Book* version, a few differences in spelling occur, such as "hundred" for "hunderd," "last" for "las" and "burned" for "burnd." My transcription of the text follows the spelling in the *Family Herald*.

This year I tried to locate the Donald McDonald identified in the editor's note as the possessor of the diary in 1963. I telephoned more than sixty McDonalds on Cooksville exchanges in the Mississauga phone book. I thank them for answering my questions. I was unable to locate the Donald McDonald I sought.

I tried to locate the archives of the *Family*

Herald to see if there was a record of authorship of the diary and to learn from whom it was purchased. There is a small archive of *Family Herald* material in the McGill University Archives but it doesn't include editorial correspondence or purchase records for 1963. I thank Robert Michel for looking there.

On the assumption that the original diary may have been placed in an archive, I asked several archivists and librarians to search their collections for it. I offer my thanks to them: Anne Goddard, National Archives of Canada; John Lutman, Regional Collection, University of Western Ontario; Stuart MacKinnon, University of Waterloo Library; Tom Belton, Archives of Ontario; Blain White, Huron County Museum; Gloria Troyer, University of Guelph Library; and Lynn Campbell, Ontario Agricultural Museum. None found the original diary and several offered helpful comments and suggestions.

Assistance in my search was also provided by Marion McGillivray of the Bruce County Historical Society, Donald J. McDonald of Brampton, Bruce Whiteman, Richard Virr and Carol Gerson. There were others to whom the matter of the diary was presented, all of whose names did not filter back to me, but whose information and ideas about it did. Bruce Krug and Ed Phelps were among them. My thanks to all of them.

It should be noted that some of the forenamed questioned the veracity of the diary. In a letter to me about the diary, Lynn Campbell wrote "My guess is that this is a piece of fiction, a parody of nineteenth century settlers' accounts written by someone who was quite familiar with the genre." One archivist commented that the fellow had too many tragedies in his life. Another likened the diary to the writings of Sarah Binks.

The authorship of the diary remains unknown to me. The question of its authenticity is unresolved. Nevertheless, its verisimilitude remains and its charm and poignancy persist.

Nelson Ball
May 1993

A Note on the Editor

NELSON BALL grew up in Huron and Bruce Counties. His interest in pioneer life began in these early years. By the age of eight, he had created "The Royal Museum of Seaforth" which was housed in his bedroom. The collection reflected his interest in biology (birds' eggs), geology (rocks and stones) and archaeology (arrow-heads), and included a cow's skull, birds' nests, coins and pioneer tools. The Museum issued a handwritten newspaper over the three years of its operation. Tours were given to school friends, and on one occasion, Nelson's entire Grade Four class visited his Museum.

Nelson Ball is a poet and bookseller. His book, *With Issa: Poems 1964-1971*, was published in 1991. He was editor and publisher of Weed Flower Press (1965-1974) and edited the literary magazines *Volume 63*, *Hyphid* and *Weed*. Since 1972, he has been an antiquarian bookseller specializing in Canadian literature. He lives in Paris, Ontario, at the forks of the Grand and Nith Rivers.